This is a fictionalised biography describing some
of the key moments (so far!) in the career of
João Félix.
Some of the events described in this book are
based upon the author's imagination and are
probably not entirely accurate representations
of what actually happened.

Tales from the Pitch
João Félix
by Harry Coninx

Published by Raven Books
An imprint of Ransom Publishing Ltd.
Unit 7, Brocklands Farm, West Meon, Hampshire GU32 1JN, UK
www.ransom.co.uk

ISBN   978 178591 979 4
First published in 2021
Reprinted 2021

A CIP catalogue record of this book is available from the British Library.

There is a reading comprehension quiz available for this book in the popular Accelerated Reader® software system. For information about ATOS, Accelerated Reader, quiz points and reading levels please visit www.renaissance.com. Accelerated Reader, AR, the Accelerated Reader Logo, and ATOS are trademarks of Renaissance Learning, Inc. and its subsidiaries, registered common law or applied for in the U.S. and other countries. Used under license.

The rights of Harry Coninx to be identified as the author and of Ben Farr to be identified as the illustrator of this Work have been asserted by them in accordance with sections 77 and 78 of the Copyright, Design and Patents Act 1988.

TALES FROM THE PITCH

JOÃO FÉLIX

HARRY CONINX

RAVEN

For my editor, Steve, a football fan in the making

CONTENTS

I

CHAMPIONS OF PORTUGAL

May 2019, Estádio da Luz, Lisbon, Portugal

Benfica v Santa Clara

João Félix looked around the changing room at his Benfica team-mates. Many of them were dripping with sweat – and that wasn't just down to the hot Portuguese sun outside.

After a gruelling season, Benfica were two points clear at the top of the Primeira Liga. Now they were about to play their final game of the season and, having been knocked out of both of Portugal's cup competitions as well as the Europa League, this was their last chance to get their hands on a trophy.

Everybody in the room knew that a two-point margin wasn't enough to guarantee them the title. To be sure of winning the league, they needed to win today.

"Come on, lads," said captain André Almeida, picking up on the tension in the room. "We've all worked too hard this season to let it slip now."

Some of the players grunted in agreement.

"And don't forget – we've been unbeaten in the league since January," manager Bruno Lage added, looking around the room. "Just treat this like any other match and it's ours. We'll win the title!"

A more determined cheer rang out from all the players – all except for João.

He just took a deep breath and pulled his socks up, trying to focus on the game ahead.

Normally Benfica would be confident of beating today's opponents, Santa Clara, but today wasn't normal.

João knew that they couldn't take anything for

granted today – not if he wanted to get his hands on his first piece of top-flight silverware.

"You ready, João?" striker Haris Seferovic´ asked him, interrupting João's thoughts.

João nodded, then followed his team-mates out onto the pitch, feeling the heat of the burning sun on his face.

The crowd was a mass of red and white and, as the players emerged from the tunnel, the noise was deafening.

But João blocked it all out and concentrated on the little voice in his head.

The longer it's 0-0, the more confident Santa Clara will become. We need an early goal.

His chance to help Benfica get that early goal came on the fifteen-minute mark.

Drifting in from the left, João flicked the ball to Andreas Samaris, who lofted it over the top to Seferovic´.

Ruthless as ever, the striker fired the ball past the Santa Clara keeper.

GOAL!

Suddenly the roaring of the Benfica fans was off the

scale. Their team were just 75 minutes from taking the title.

The minutes that followed the goal were nervy. Santa Clara had a few good chances, but luckily for Benfica they weren't able to make any of them count.

Then Benfica got their next opportunity. João had helped Benfica get their first goal – now he wanted to double their lead with a goal of his own.

The ball bobbled and bounced into the box, before landing at his feet. João instantly faked a shot with his left, before cutting the ball onto his right foot.

The goal opened up in front of him and a split-second later the ball hit the roof of the net.

GOAL!

Now it was 2-0!

João sprinted to the corner, sliding along the floor in celebration, his arms folded across his chest.

In the stands the fans were going wild for their main man, a player who'd been dubbed "the heir to Ronaldo".

As João celebrated his goal with the Benfica fans, he couldn't help but think back to the dark days, only a few years ago, when he'd been released by Porto's youth academy and told that he didn't have what it took to become a professional football player.

He'd even given up on his dream of becoming a professional player.

Yet here he was, not just fulfilling that dream, but scoring goals for the best club in Portugal.

Not long after João's goal, Rafa Silva added a third for Benfica and, in the stands, it looked as if the title celebrations had already begun.

Surely Benfica couldn't lose now?

At half-time, some of the Benfica players were already celebrating in the dressing room.

Lage tried to calm them down. "It's not won yet, lads," he said. "Don't lose focus out there. Crazier things have happened in football! Let's make sure we keep up the intensity!"

But he needn't have worried.

Ten minutes into the second half, Benfica scored their fourth.

Álex Grimaldo burst down the left-hand side and whipped in a brilliant cross which Seferović flicked into the back of the net.

"Even the gaffer can't say it isn't done now!" João laughed, turning to Rafa Silva as they celebrated with the striker.

Santa Clara got a late consolation, but it wasn't enough.

When João was subbed off after 70 minutes, the players all knew the job was done. Benfica were going to win the game – and the league.

João embraced his manager on the touchline.

"You were brilliant today, João!" Lage grinned.

João just smiled at his manager, then sat back to watch the rest of the match.

The remainder of the game was really just a victory lap for Benfica – they were overwhelming, quite untouchable.

When the referee blew the full-time whistle, João jumped up, looking up at the sky in celebration. For the first time in his life, he was a Portuguese champion.

During the ceremony that followed, he barely looked away from the trophy that was glinting magnificently in the bright sunshine.

"I'll never get used to this feeling," André Almeida

remarked, as he held the trophy in his arms. Almeida was now a veteran of five title wins – this was João's first.

"I don't think I ever will," João laughed, still staring at the trophy.

Deep down, he knew that this wasn't going to be his last trophy.

He was only just getting started.

2
JOÃO'S DRIVE

May 2010, Félix family car, Porto, Portugal

Ten-year-old João closed his eyes and swallowed hard.

Being in the car for so long was starting to make him feel really sick.

" 'You alright, João?" his dad asked him from the driver's seat. "Not far now – we're almost there."

João nodded and thought about where they were going.

Porto Academy.

The wave of nausea faded slightly as a small, excited smile spread across his face.

João had been with the academy for almost two years now – and he still absolutely loved it.

He loved the quality of training the academy gave him, and he loved the fact that all the other boys there were almost as obsessed with football as he was.

And, perhaps, most of all, he loved the fact he could say that Porto, one of *the* legendary teams in football, was *his* team.

The one problem with it all, though, was the drive. João most definitely did *not* love the drive.

He opened his eyes to look at the small clock on the dashboard. He and his dad had already been in the car for an hour and a half. After training today, they'd have to do the same drive all over again, to get back home to Viseu.

João and his dad did this three-hour round trip to training twice a week, plus all the travel to get to and from the weekend matches.

It was exhausting.

João often thought about leaving Porto and going back to playing with a smaller team near his parents' home in Viseu. It would avoid all this travelling.

But then he'd think about one of his idols – Kaka. He'd joined São Paulo at the age of eight, and by the time he was 19 he'd moved across the world to join Milan.

To be the best, João knew he had to be playing with the best. So he always decided to stay at Porto.

"So, who are you going to play like today, João?" his dad asked him, trying to take João's mind off his car-sickness. "Rui Costa? Or Figo? Ronaldo?"

His dad knew that these were João's three favourite players.

"I don't know," said João, grinning broadly. "Maybe I'll just play as João Félix today. I mean, one day I'm going to win the league with Porto – I'm going to be a Portuguese Champion! So people will need to know how *I* play!"

His dad grinned as they pulled into the academy car park.

Minutes later, João was in his element, being coached on the importance of a perfect touch.

"Remember," the coach, Alberto, said to him, pacing up ahead. "It's good to be fit, but if you can pass – if you can control the ball, move it on to someone else and then find space – *then* you don't need to be the fastest on the pitch."

João concentrated on the ball that was being lofted towards him by Diogo Dalot, one of his friends at the academy. He met the ball with his foot and killed it dead.

"Think about Barcelona," Alberto continued, still making his point. "How often do you see Xavi or Iniesta sprinting around, chasing the ball? You don't. They control the ball, pass it on, then find the space."

"What about Messi?" João asked. "He does a lot of sprinting, surely?"

"He does short bursts of sprinting, I'll give you that," the coach admitted. "But a lot of the time he walks around, finding little pockets of space where he can pick the ball up and run at players. It's all about working smart, not working hard!"

João liked this approach. He stopped trying to fight for the ball from the defenders all the time and learned to saved his energy, waiting for the right chance when he could run at the defence.

João loved his training sessions – the friendships, the learning and the sheer pleasure of playing football.

But each session seemed to fly by in no time at all.

And then João had to face the dreaded long journey home.

3

THE PORTO PROJECT

May 2012, Porto Academy, Porto, Portugal

João flicked the ball around the outstretched leg of the defender and moved it onto his left foot.

In the split-second that followed, he sized up the goalkeeper's position and whipped the ball with his foot, curling it into the top corner of the goal.

Even though it was only a practice game, he was elated to see the ball ripple the back of the net.

He spent the remainder of the match making it happen again … and again … and again.

"Not bad, João," laughed Diogo. "But have you given up on passing? I'm sure a few other players wouldn't mind scoring one or two as well."

João grinned. He'd been training at the Porto Academy for four years now, and he knew he was improving all the time.

He and Diogo had become good mates too, but it was a pity that João lived so far away. It meant that they could only meet up in training or at matches.

"That was great stuff today, João," Alberto said, ruffling the youngster's mop of hair as João came off the pitch at full time. "Your ability on the ball is just getting better and better."

Then the coach turned and shouted towards the group of parents gathered at the edge of the pitch.

"Carlos – Félix's dad! Could you come over here, please?"

Alberto's shout was so unexpected it almost made João jump. Anyway, why would Alberto want to speak to his dad?

"Listen guys," Alberto said, once João's dad had come over and joined them. "I want to talk to you about an opportunity we've got. You know João is an exceptional talent – that's no secret. In fact, he's just the kind of talent we're looking for for our elite player project."

Exceptional talent. Elite. João was practically glowing at the sound of these words.

"Now, I've never heard either of you complain about the drive you make to get here," Alberto went on, "but I know it must be a huge burden for both of you. João is easily good enough to join our elite project. And if he did, he could move into the youth accommodation here. That would cut out all that driving."

João suddenly felt his stomach lurch. The thought of moving out of his home made him feel just like he did on long car journeys – as if he was going to be sick.

He was only twelve, after all!

João listened nervously as his dad thanked Alberto for his kind words and for the offer.

"Give us a bit of time to have a think about it as a family," Carlos told him. "Then we'll get back to you."

As they headed back to the car park in the warm evening air, João's mind was racing.

He liked all the lads here at the academy, but there was no way they could replace his mum, his dad and his brother, Hugo.

Of course he loved coming to this place to train, to play football and to learn – but none of that was enough to make it his home.

But the sight of his dad unlocking their little car made João think of him too.

His dad had been dedicating his evenings to bringing João here for almost five years now. This way, at least, he could have a break from that.

Besides, thought João, he'd lost hours of his own time to the drives as well. Hours that he could have spent playing football, getting him closer to his dream.

Sitting in the car, João turned to his dad.

"Dad, I think I should do it, you know. I think I should move here."

4
FAR FROM HOME

April 2014, Porto Academy accommodation,
Porto, Portugal

The Porto Academy accommodation was just a stone's throw from the club's famous Estádio do Dragão stadium and João often found himself looking out of the window at the impressive building.

João had been both excited and nervous to be moving to the academy. He'd never lived outside Viseu before – or lived away from his parents.

The day they'd dropped him off had been tough.

As they'd left, João hadn't said anything, afraid that if he spoke he'd only end up crying.

Watching his parents and his brother driving away, João had just stood there, wondering if he'd made the wrong choice.

His homesickness had never gone away. The promise of one day playing at Porto's famous stadium was all he had to help him curb the feelings of homesickness.

The move into the academy accommodation had turned out to be harder than he'd ever imagined, and he missed so many things from home.

He desperately missed playing with his brother, he missed his bedroom, his mum's cooking, and – he hated to admit it – he even missed the car rides with his dad to and from training.

There had been many times over the past year when it had all become too much, and he'd rung home in tears, asking his parents to come and pick him up.

"I'll come and get you," his dad had always said, "but

after that, I'll never drive you there again. You're going to have to live with your decision. So, before you say anything, make sure it's really what you want to do."

And every time, João had decided to stay at the academy. He would stick with football. As long as that was on track, everything else was worthwhile.

"You coming, João?"

The voice interrupted his thoughts.

João turned from the window and saw all the other boys slowly filing along the corridor.

João nodded and ran back to his room to grab his boots. The academy had a friendly with a rival youth team set up for today, which was probably the perfect thing to help him forget about home.

Boots in hand, João walked towards the changing room where the other boys were already getting kitted up.

Almost at the door, he overheard a few voices discussing today's friendly. He recognised the voices as those of his coaches, and he couldn't avoid stopping to listen when he heard his name being mentioned.

"Félix. How about we play him as the number 9 today?" said one voice.

"No, no," came the reply. "That kid would snap like a twig."

João's heart dropped.

In the days after overhearing that conversation, João suddenly began to notice how much his fellow youth players had shot up.

While he'd been feeling homesick and thinking about his home comforts, it seemed as if all the other boys had been busy growing taller – and filling out.

It suddenly dawned on João that he was now one of the shortest, skinniest boys in his age group.

But for all that, he was still a quick and skilful dribbler and, when he saw his name in the starting line-up for a match against Braga's youth side later that week, he knew he needed to remind the coaches of his skills.

He badly needed to make this opportunity count.

His coaches played him out on the wing for the game, and from the first minute João knew he had the beating of his full-back.

"Get it out to me, guys!" he yelled to his team-mates.

They got the ball out to him and he flicked it past the full-back and raced on towards the goal, the ball at his feet.

As João got into the box he saw the centre-back approaching, and he smiled at the chance to show off his skills.

Sure enough, he skipped past him – but as he did so the centre-back barged him, sending him flying to the ground.

"Foul! Penalty!" João called in frustration from the floor.

But the ref ignored his protests and waved the game on.

"You need to eat a few more sandwiches, kid," the centre-back smirked, running back up the pitch.

João looked to his team-mates, hoping to get some support, but they had all looked away.

Nobody was backing him.

He picked himself up and jogged back into the game, but just a few minutes later he was subbed off.

João stormed over to the bench, feeling a strange mix

of emotions. He felt angry, but at the same time he felt embarrassed, frustrated, upset, homesick and tired.

Everything just felt like it was too much – and João didn't know to handle it.

As he sat on the bench and watched the other boys carrying on with the game, the whole idea of being one of the top players here, of having been asked to join the elite player project, felt like a distant memory, like a bad joke.

Then, suddenly, it struck him.

He wasn't going to make it as a footballer. It was as simple as that. It had all been a waste.

It was over.

5
AND ... RELEASE

June 2015, João's childhood home, Viseu, Portugal

"I just want to stay here," João said, fighting back tears.

He was back at home with his parents for the weekend, and he couldn't bear the thought of tearing himself away from these familiar surroundings to head back to the academy.

"I don't want to go back to Porto," João said, looking up at his mum and dad as the tears welled up again.

He nearly went on to tell them that he wasn't even sure that Porto would have him back next year, but he managed to stop himself. He was just too ashamed to say it out loud.

The club had already made it pretty clear anyway. João wasn't getting any game time in the youth competitions, and the coaches obviously didn't see a future for him.

And the worst thing was, he just didn't care any more. His love for football had gone.

João's mum went over and put an arm around him. She'd been worried about her son ever since he'd moved to Porto.

João had always been homesick when they'd spoken on the phone, but she'd always thought that he'd get through it.

But over the past few months, whenever they'd phoned each other, she'd noticed that something had changed in her son's voice.

And now that he was here, she could see that the spark in his eye – the spark he'd had ever since he'd been a toddler kicking a ball – had gone.

As his mum tried to comfort him, the phone rang. His dad went to pick it up.

"Hello, sir," he said, walking into the kitchen, out of earshot.

João tensed. His dad didn't call anyone "sir" apart from the director of football at the academy.

"I see," he heard his dad say.

His dad's tone told João everything he needed to know.

Porto had released him.

Whatever had been left of João's dream of being a footballer was now well and truly over.

6
EAGLE EYES

July 2015, Benfica Academy, Lisbon, Portugal

João stood awkwardly on the Benfica pitch, looking around and feeling a little unsure.

When his parents had suggested to him that he come here today, he hadn't been entirely convinced.

"I think you should give football one more chance," his mum had urged. "Every club is different – and Benfica Academy might be a better fit for you."

"And anyway, I've always preferred Benfica to Porto," his dad had joked, trying to lighten the mood.

Eventually João had given in and agreed to give it a go.

So now here he was, standing amongst a group of teenage boys in front of a gaggle of coaches, none of whom had even given him a second glance.

João felt no pressure as he stood there waiting.

But he was painfully aware of how skinny he looked next to the other players on the pitch.

The coaches started the session by leading the boys in a warm-up, then got them set up to play a game.

With a ball at his feet, all of João's hesitancy about coming here today suddenly evaporated.

He got himself right into the game. Every pass he made found a team-mate, every shot found the top corner – and the defenders couldn't touch him.

And what's more, he enjoyed every minute of it. It was the most fun he'd had on a pitch in what felt like … forever.

At the sound of the final whistle João looked up to see the coaches huddled together on the touchline, eyes fixed on him while they muttered to each other under their breath.

Instantly he felt very self-conscious. He dropped his gaze, looking away. They were probably thinking about how small he was, he thought, how skinny.

How he was wasting everyone's time by just turning up today.

How could such a little kid ever think he could become a professional player?

Then one of the coaches stepped forward.

"Time to take a break, lads," he said to the group, before looking down at his clipboard. "But, uh, João? João Félix? Can I have a word with you?"

João shuffled over, sure he was about to be sent home. He just hoped they didn't embarrass him in front of the others.

"Great to meet you, João. I wondered if you wanted to kick a ball about with me, have a chat?"

João was taken aback by the odd request, but he nodded and followed the man to an empty corner of the pitch, where they started knocking the ball back and forth.

"I'm Renato Paiva," the man said warmly. "I coach the youth players here at Benfica. I know from what your parents told me that you've had a bit of a tough time recently."

João nodded. "I was with Porto," he said quietly. "But they thought I was too small."

"I see. Well, then someone had better let Messi know he has a problem," Renato replied with a wink.

João smiled, then started to kick the ball with a little more purpose.

"With all due respect, João, I think Porto made a big mistake letting you go," Renato went on. "And I'm not just saying that because they're our old rivals. Your technical ability on the ball – well, it's … "

Renato paused, looking for the words. " … out of the ordinary. And in that game you played just now, I also saw a real football intelligence. Creativity, too."

João smiled at the praise and they continued kicking the ball back and forth in silence, Renato sometimes sending it wide, forcing João to control it.

After a minute he spoke again.

"You know, João, I think you should give it a go here.

I've got a feeling we can help you show Porto that they've missed a trick with you."

7

B FOR BENFICA

September 2016, Benfica Academy, Lisbon, Portugal

"How does number 79 work for you?"

João wanted to tell Hélder Cristóvão that any number would work for him, but he couldn't find any words, so he just nodded eagerly.

A place on Benfica's B team – a team brimming with talents like Rúben Dias, Luka Jović and Zé Gomes – was a huge deal, even though João knew he deserved it.

He'd been at Benfica Academy for over a year now, and he could see why it was heralded as one of the best on the planet.

Under the eye of expert coaches who were producing some of the biggest superstars in the game, João was playing the best football of his life, and his confidence was steadily getting back to where it used to be, back in those early days.

This time the move hadn't affected him and his homesickness was long gone. Everyone here believed in him, and that made the academy feel like a second home to him, in a way that Porto never had.

If Porto had been a nightmare, Benfica was a dream.

There was an emphasis at Benfica on passing and holding on to the ball. It didn't matter that João was slight and skinny.

"Do you want me to join in on the running drills?" João had asked, after one particularly exhausting session.

"No, no, not if you can't do it, João," Renato had replied. "Take a breather instead."

It was a far cry from the treatment he'd received at Porto. Benfica didn't want to overwork their players, or make them do things they weren't good at. Rather, they wanted to get the best out of all their players, to mould them into a team.

And the number 79 shirt was the proof it was working.

João was already playing in the UEFA Youth League, and now here he was, being given a shirt for Benfica B.

In many European countries a lot of the top clubs had two teams in the league. Their second team, the B team, was effectively the reserve team, but they got to play in the league as a team in their own right.

So joining a B team was a great opportunity because, instead of just playing against other B teams, you got to play against other first teams in the league as well.

"Well, number 79 it is," Hélder said. "I can't promise you you'll come on – but if you do, you should know that you'll be the youngest player ever to make their debut for Benfica B."

João was blown away.

"Are you sure I'm strong enough?" he asked. To his delight, he'd grown taller in the past year, but he was still on the skinny side. "D'you think I'll be able to hold people off?"

"Like we always say, João, it's not about build or strength," Hélder reassured him. "It's about balance. Messi gets knocks, but he stays on his feet. You've got the same knack as him. You'll do brilliantly."

João wasn't convinced. "But I'm always getting knocked over," he said.

"Not as much as you think," Hélder replied. "You're brilliant at it and you haven't even realised. Anyway, if anyone barges you hard enough so you go over, then you stay down – and win us a free kick. Alright?"

It was an away match and Benfica B were playing SC Freamunde.

João sat on the subs bench, spending half his time watching the game and the other half watching Hélder for any sign that he might be considering bringing him on.

It had been a drab game and the score was still 0-0, so João was just beginning to give up hope. They weren't going to risk bringing on a young player if the game was still in the balance like that.

But then, after 80 minutes, Hélder turned to look at the bench and beckoned him over.

"Go out there and get a feel for it, João," he said.

A few minutes later João was completing his first pass in a senior game. He felt on top of the world knowing that, of all the great players who had come through the ranks of Benfica B, he was making history as the youngest.

His ten minutes on the pitch felt more like ten seconds, and he was disappointed to hear the final whistle.

But he walked off the pitch with one thing clear in his mind.

His love for football was well and truly back – and he was hungrier to succeed than he'd ever been before.

8
THE REAL THING

April 2017, Centre Sportif de Colovray, Nyon, Switzerland
UEFA Youth League, Real Madrid U19 v Benfica U19

"We can do this!" roared captain Rúben Dias to the players sitting in the dressing room before the game. "Win this and we're in the final! Don't let Real Madrid spook you. On our day we can beat them easily – and today is our day! Now, let's go!"

The Benfica U19 players responded with loud cheers as they made their way out onto the pitch.

João began the game behind striker Zé Gomes. It gave him the room he loved to find space and create opportunities.

Although the Real Madrid team wasn't packed full of stars, João knew they had some quality players and it was going to be a tough game.

After just five minutes Gedson Fernandes whipped a low cross into the box, where João was lurking, completely unmarked.

Even though he had his back to goal, João was able to spin and backheel it past the keeper.

GOAL!

João sprinted to the sidelines, where he was quickly mobbed by his celebrating team-mates.

"That was genius, João!" Gedson shouted, chasing after him.

"Now let's go and get another," João replied, pushing him away.

Benfica did get a second just ten minutes later, Jota twisting and firing a shot at goal. The effort looked as though it was heading straight for the keeper's arms, but he fumbled it and it slipped into the back of the net.

Benfica were two up after a just a quarter of an hour. Everything seemed to be going their way today.

Two minutes later, Diogo Gonçalves burst away down the left-hand side.

"I'm free!" João shouted, making a late run into the box.

Gonçalves cut it back and João met it with the side of his right foot, slamming the ball into the top of the net.

"Let's get five or six now!" João shouted, getting a little carried away.

But Real Madrid weren't done yet. Dani Gómez got one back before half-time and then Real grabbed a second in the second half.

Benfica were now under the cosh, their 3-0 lead reduced to just a single goal.

For Benfica it was all about defence in the second half. Real Madrid were dominant and there was little that João could do.

He was replaced by David Tavares with 20 minutes of the game left, and watched anxiously from the sidelines, praying they had enough to win.

The game was in added time now, each minute passing like an eternity.

But suddenly Benfica broke.

Real Madrid had most of their players forward and Benfica had acres of space to charge into.

Diogo Mendes rattled the post with a shot, but the ball came back to Jota, who poked it home.

GOAL! 4-2!

That was surely the game done and dusted.

A minute later it was confirmed. Benfica were into the final!

"Enjoy this one, lads!" Hélder said, gathering all the players round him before returning to the dressing room. "You won't get many opportunities to *play* Real Madrid, let alone beat them, so hold on to this one!"

For João in particular, this was a win to remember. They'd played Real Madrid, they'd won – and he had put two of the goals past them.

9
GOAL-GETTER

January 2018, Caixa Futebol Campus, Lisbon, Portugal
Benfica B v FC Famalicão

Finding himself through on goal, João glanced towards the linesman. He thought he was offside, but the flag stayed down.

Turning to face the goal, João looked at the Famalicão goalkeeper. He'd come charging out to close João down, so João took a deep breath, steadied himself – and neatly rolled the ball past him.

GOAL!

"Yes! João!" Keaton Parks screamed. "That was amazing!"

But João wasn't done yet. He was sure that he'd get more than just one goal in this game.

After all, he'd been playing for both Benfica B and Benfica U19s for the last season and a half, and he was going from strength to strength.

He'd found the net against the youth teams of Dynamo Kiev, PSV Eindhoven – even Real Madrid.

He knew he could get another here.

Sure enough, in the second half he once more found himself charging towards goal, this time opting to dink the ball over the keeper.

GOAL!

Then, as Nuno Santos slipped the ball towards both João and striker Zé Gomes, João made it clear that he wanted it.

"João's!" he bellowed, letting Zé know it was his.

With his first touch João slipped it neatly past the keeper.

GOAL!

That was three! João had his hat-trick – the first of his professional career!

"You quiet kids always end up being monsters on the pitch," Nuno laughed, slapping João on the back.

João just grinned, quite aware of how his determination would often possess him during a match.

Especially as he was currently set on achieving one goal, something that a hat-trick was sure to help him accomplish.

Breaking into the Benfica first team.

10
READY OR NOT

August 2018, Benfica training ground, Lisbon, Portugal

Three minutes against Boavista in the Primeira Liga, then ten minutes against Salonika in a Champions League qualifier.

João's efforts had indeed got him a call-up from the Benfica first-team manager, Rui Vitoria, and his first tastes of game time with the team had shown him how fierce top-level Portuguese football was.

At first, João thought it was just because the players in this division were fitter. But he soon realised that it was a lot more complicated than that …

Benfica B played in the Liga Portugal 2 – Portugal's second division. If, in the second division, you had five seconds to make a decision, in the Primeira Liga you had just one.

The players around you were also a lot more organised and, nine times out of ten, the split-second decisions they made were the right ones.

They just knew whether to shoot or to cross, whether to close someone down or to back off and let them come to you.

That was why the pace of the games in the Primeira Liga was so high. Everyone was making the right decisions – and taking no time at all to think about them.

It was exhausting. And so was the training.

And today was no exception.

João had always struggled with training drills. He wanted to be out on the pitch with a ball, not going through these boring routines.

He knew it wasn't made easier by the fact that he was smaller than some of the other players – and he couldn't forget what Alberto had told them at Porto, about fitness not being the most important thing on the pitch.

If he was honest, João was hoping that Alberto had been right about the fitness thing.

João looked up to see Benfica's star left-back Álex Grimaldo grinning at him.

"Hey, João, you look like you enjoy these drills as much as I do," he laughed.

João did his best to look as if he wasn't finding it that hard.

"You look like you're struggling with them a bit, João," Álex went on. "When you're doing these drills, just like when you're out on the pitch, try to listen to your body and work *with* it, not against it. That makes it a lot easier. It's a great feeling when it finally clicks and it all comes together. That's when you really move up a level."

João still didn't like drills, but he was grateful for the advice, and he felt better knowing that even the great Álex Grimaldo had struggled with training.

"So you're not going to give up, right?" Álex continued. "Because I want you on the wing with me."

João shook his head. He'd almost given up on his dream once. He wasn't going to do it again, whatever the world of football threw at him.

"No, I'll be there."

"Good, because it's almost derby day," Álex said with a wicked smile. "We'll need everyone at their best."

II
DERBY DAY

August 2018, Estádio da Luz, Lisbon, Portugal
Benfica v Sporting

João sat on the bench, still overwhelmed by the atmosphere.

The stadium was all Benfica, the only exception being a small, green pocket of Sporting fans high up in one corner.

He'd never witnessed a crowd like it.

The stands seemed to be just a sea of arms, flags and

scarves, and he could barely hear his own thoughts over the noise of the fans, chanting and singing songs about the hard-fought game that was being played out on the pitch.

They were half-way through the second half and, though there were a number of talented players on the pitch, neither side had really been able to express themselves.

They were deadlocked at 0-0 and, as was often the way with local derbies, the game was marred by a number of niggling fouls and challenges.

With every second that passed, things seemed to be getting more tense on the pitch.

João had started on the bench, and a tiny part of him was actually afraid that he'd be asked to go on in front of this huge crowd of excited fans.

But he ignored that. Showing up on occasions like this was his chance to cement himself in this first team. If the opportunity came, he would take it with both hands.

It wasn't until the 60th minute that the game turned, when Sporting's Freddy Montero went down in the box.

From where he was sitting João couldn't see what had happened, but he did see the referee point to the penalty spot.

Portugal legend Nani dispatched it coolly to give Sporting a 1-0 lead.

Benfica were now losing to their local rivals – and on their own turf as well.

Not long after Nani's goal, the moment João was waiting for came.

Rui beckoned him over.

"It looks like there's a lot of pressure out there, but there isn't really," the manager bellowed, trying to keep his voice calm at the same time. "Most of it is just bluster – so don't let it distract you. Now, I don't expect you to win this, but go out there and give it your best shot. Do something unpredictable."

João struggled at first with the pace and the energy of the game, but gradually he got into it with a little flick here, a good touch there.

And then, with five minutes left on the clock, he found himself making a burst into the box.

The ball had gone wide to Rafa Silva and João knew

that he was in a good position to win a header if the ball came in.

It suddenly occurred to him that he'd never been great at headers, but there was no point thinking about things like that here. He was a Primeira Liga player now – he had to trust his instincts.

Then he remembered his conversation in training with Álex Grimaldo, about everything coming together and things suddenly going up a level.

"Rafa!" João roared, over the immense din of the crowd. "Back post!"

The ball flew in and João leapt into the air, rising high above the defender in front of him. All he needed to do was make contact.

He did, heading the ball down to the ground and towards the corner. It evaded the desperate lunge of the keeper and nestled in the back of the net.

GOAL!

A shiver ran through João's body as the noise in the stadium somehow reached new heights.

He didn't really know what to do to celebrate, so he found himself sprinting towards the fans, jumping up and down and punching the air – doing every kind of celebration he'd ever seen a footballer do – while his team-mates mobbed him.

For João the final minutes of the game were a blur.

Benfica couldn't get the winner, but considering how close they'd come to defeat, it felt like a victory.

"I told you to do something unpredictable," Rui grinned, slapping João on the back as he came off at full time. "But I've got to say, a header from you is definitely not something I'd have predicted."

João nodded, delighted with his goal.

"I imagine you'll want to go and ring your parents," added Rui. "Well, you might also want to let them know that you're the youngest player ever to score in the Lisbon derby."

Rui was right. João couldn't wait to tell his mum and dad about the game.

This incredible day wouldn't have happened without their support.

João looked at his Benfica team-mates coming off the pitch and suddenly remembered those long car trips to and from training with his dad.

He could feel the tears welling up again.

This time, he was here and it was real. And this time, he knew it wasn't going to go away.

12

MEETING BRUNO

January 2019, Benfica training ground, Lisbon, Portugal

João walked into the Benfica manager's office knowing that Rui Vitoria wouldn't be there, but it was still a bit of a shock to see a new face sitting at the manager's desk.

The past few months had been tough for Benfica, and being beaten recently by Portimonense had been the final straw for the club's board.

Rui had been sacked as Benfica's manager – and Bruno Lage had been appointed in his place.

"I know a new face can take a little getting used to," Bruno said kindly, picking up on João's expression as the young player hovered in the doorway.

Bruno gestured for him to come in and take a seat, and João did so.

"How do you feel about the change of manager?" Bruno asked, looking directly at him.

"I'm sad to see Rui go. He gave me my debut – and I know myself what it feels like to be released. But … "

João paused for a moment, considering how open he should be with his new manager.

Bruno's smile encouraged him to continue.

"Well, he wasn't really starting me," João continued. "I was just a bench player. I was out for a month with an ankle injury, I know, but all the same I thought the fact that I had two goals by September, one in a derby, would have counted for something."

"This is how it is in football," Bruno said, leaning back casually in his chair. "Sometimes you can be doing everything right, but if a manager isn't keen on young players, then ... well, he isn't keen on young players. That's it. You won't change his mind."

João nodded. He desperately wanted to ask Bruno how *he* felt about using younger players – but he didn't have to. Bruno just carried on talking.

"I happen to think that it's the young players that make great teams what they are," he said. "It's where the magic and the energy comes from. That feeds the rest of the team."

Bruno paused and looked at João, then continued. "This past year I've actually been in charge of Benfica B. They miss you over there, João – and when I watch footage of you, I can see why. You're a natural talent. That's why I want you playing your natural game, starting just behind our striker. Every match."

João couldn't believe what he was hearing.

He was going to be the main man in Benfica's attack! He was even going to be playing in his preferred position, in the middle, not out on the wing where he'd been played recently.

And he had a manager who, it seemed, really believed in him.

João collected his thoughts as he looked at the manager opposite him.

Bruno already seemed so comfortable in his new surroundings. He seemed so confident about where he was going to take the club.

It made João feel the same way.

"I won't let you down, boss. I'll get us back in the title race."

13
JOÃO'S REVENGE

March 2019, Estádio Do Dragão, Porto, Portugal
Benfica v Porto

No words could describe how it felt to be lining up in Porto's tunnel.

João had spent so much of his childhood and his teenage years believing that he'd end up playing here. It was something he'd clung onto, to help him get through his move away from home.

And now he was finally here, but he wasn't playing

for Porto as he'd dreamed. He was playing against them, playing with a different team – one that just happened to be one of Porto's biggest rivals.

He took a deep breath. He was ready to show them what he'd made of himself with Bruno's faith and support.

Indeed, João and his manager had both been true to their word.

Bruno had put João in the starting eleven for every match, and João had become central to the success that now saw Benfica back in the title race.

Despite the fact it was still only March and it was still only his first proper season in Portugal's top flight, João was already on 10 goals.

As he stood in the player's tunnel, he could hear some of the Porto players whispering to each other as they looked across at him.

"That's João Félix. He's the one to watch. I'm glad I'm not marking him."

"He used to train here, at the academy."

"No way! Then how did we lose him to Benfica?"

"No idea. But the word is, PSG, Arsenal, Man U and

Barcelona have all got their eyes on him. So he may not be around for long anyway."

It seemed that the Porto fans knew his history with their club as well, and as the game kicked off they booed every touch he got.

When Porto took the lead early in the game, through Adrián López, the jeering from the Porto fans only went up a notch.

But João was now more experienced in handling these kinds of situations, and he used the crowd's response to fire himself up.

So when Haris Seferovic' won the ball back from a Porto defender and raced forward, João was ready.

'Haris! Square it!' João bellowed over the din of the Porto fans.

Haris did just that. João controlled it instantly, then slammed the ball past the Porto keeper, Casillas.

GOAL!

As he watched the ball cross the line, João thought back to that day when he'd first come to Benfica, and Renato Paiva had told him that they could help him show Porto what a mistake they'd made.

Well here it was. This was the proof they'd made a mistake.

João roared at the sky, then sprinted towards the corner, sliding on his knees in front of the Porto fans.

His team-mates joined him in the corner, half-hugging him, half-pulling him back, eager to get the game restarted so they could win it.

Sure enough, Rafa Silva grabbed the winner in the second half and Benfica sealed a crucial 2-1 win.

The win put Benfica at the top of the table, with the title almost in their hands.

In João's very first season as a professional player, he was close to his first title.

14

"RONALDO'S HEIR"

June 2019, Cidade do Futebol, Oeiras, Lisbon, Portugal

João knew that the call-up to a national team was an incredible moment for any football player anywhere, but for João, as part of a legendary footballing nation like Portugal, it meant something else too.

It meant sharing a pitch with the likes of Pepe, João Moutinho ... and Cristiano Ronaldo.

João would no doubt have made his Portugal debut

earlier in the season, but he'd had a few injuries which had prevented him playing.

Nevertheless, his impressive performance throughout the previous season had secured him a place in the Portugal squad for the UEFA Nations League – and he was down to start in Portugal's next game, the semi-final against Switzerland.

As the players started going through their warm-up routines at Portugal's shiny new City of Football training camp outside Lisbon, João noticed Cristiano coming over.

The two had spoken briefly before, but that didn't mean that João was still anything less than terrified of talking to him.

Then João reminded himself. He was now a Portuguese champion, with 20 goals and 11 assists in his first season. Surely he could do this. He could talk to Cristiano Ronaldo.

"Hey, João. Welcome to the best team in the world," said Cristiano, his face beaming.

João wasn't sure what to say, so he just kept quiet.

"So you're the one everyone's talking about,"

Cristiano continued. "Portugal's new rising star! I even read somewhere that you're the heir to 'the great Ronaldo'."

João just grinned.

"Well, I'm not retiring for a long time yet, so I don't need any heirs. But let's see what *you've* got to offer against Switzerland. See you on the pitch, João!"

And with that Cristiano was off, leaving João to watch him walk into the dressing room, drawing admiring glances from players and coaches alike.

The Switzerland match saw a completely awestruck João spending a lot of the game watching Cristiano – who was indeed at the top of his game.

Twenty-five minutes in, Portugal won a free kick which Ronaldo blasted into the top corner in his typical fashion.

Cristiano's confidence, as well as the quality of the Portugal team, inspired João to play at his very best, but the pace of senior international games was high and he found himself subbed off before the end of the match.

He'd loved to have done more on his debut, but watching Ronaldo score another two late goals to rescue Portugal and seal a 3-1 win was a reward in itself.

As João followed the superstar into the dressing room at full time, he wasn't sure he deserved the title of Ronaldo's "heir" just yet – but he knew would get there.

In time, he would make his nation proud.

In the dressing room João picked up his phone, expecting to see a few messages from his family and friends.

In amongst them was a message from Bruno.

> Great work João! Want to see you using everything you learn from those guys next season. We want a good Champions League run!

It wasn't the first message he'd received about the upcoming season. Rumours of interest from clubs all over Europe in signing him were still rife.

He knew that Benfica were trying to make it clear to any interested clubs that João should stay at Benfica for the next season.

A big move would come, no doubt, but they were saying that now was too soon.

As he changed out of his kit, surrounded by so many Portuguese legends who were playing in the greatest leagues in the world, João wondered whether Benfica were right about that.

15
ONE FOR MILLIONS

July 2019, Benfica training ground, Lisbon, Portugal

Benfica's and Bruno's predictions had come to pass.

It wasn't one of the Premier League giants, or Real Madrid, or Barcelona – but a club had put in a bid for João.

"Atlético Madrid have met your release clause," João's agent told him. "They're offering 126 million euros."

João had been speechless many times before in his career, but this shocked him more than anything.

His agent was obviously taken aback as well, as he stumbled as he tried to explain what this meant.

"It would make you, well, the fourth most expensive player ever. It would also be Benfica's biggest transfer ever – and Atlético's most expensive signing ever."

João's agent paused, letting it sink it. "And you're only 19, so – in terms of a fee for a teenager – it's the second highest of all time."

João just sat there. The fee was crazy, obviously, but what did it all really mean? It meant that he'd be playing football for Atlético Madrid.

How did he feel about *that*?

"It's up to you now, João," his agent said. "Benfica have accepted it – they can't turn down that kind of money. But if you don't want to go, nobody can make you."

João needed to think it over carefully.

He loved Benfica. They'd picked him up at his lowest point and they'd made him the player he was today.

And he'd heard many tales of young players moving

to the big clubs too soon. They were all reasons to stay where he was.

Moving clubs would be a risk, no doubt.

But then he thought back to Cristiano, who could boast league titles in England, in Spain and in Italy …

João wanted that too – and he'd come too far to stop now. He knew that if he wanted it, he'd have to make it happen.

And he knew it wouldn't happen at Benfica.

His last move had been a free transfer after a release. His next move would make history.

16
ATLETI AND THE DARK ARTS

August 2019, Atlético Madrid training ground
Madrid, Spain

João had only been at Atlético a few weeks, but he could already see why manager Diego Simeone was such a cult hero, loved and adored by both the club's fans and its players.

He was charismatic and fun to listen to – but there was always an intense look in his eyes, as if he might just snap at any moment.

It certainly made it hard to take your eyes off him.

And he wasn't the only one at Atlético who shared that kind of intense gaze. Diego Costa, Koke, José Giménez, Saúl – they were all charismatic and super-friendly off the pitch.

But when a match started – even if it was just a practice game on the training ground – then they turned into something quite frightening.

João was actually surprised that they hadn't injured him yet, given the ferocity with which they played even their practice games.

"João!" Simeone's voice boomed across the training ground as the manager strode towards him.

Up close, Simeone was an intimidating presence.

"Me and Costa were just running through some training drills," he continued. "I want you to join in."

Diego Costa was one of the best players in the world and he had a reputation for being unpredictable.

The drill wasn't one João had done at Benfica. It was all about positioning and off-the-ball work, and he barely got a touch. The only time he did get the ball, he was clattered by José Giménez.

"Woah!" he said, looking round at the rest of the team. Who tackled like that in a training session?

But nobody raised an eyebrow and the training session just carried on as before.

Diego Costa sauntered over to João, a big grin on his face. "On your feet, kid," he growled, hauling João up by his arm. "You need to toughen up here."

It was a hard lesson to learn and these big personalities were a lot for João to cope with, especially on top of dealing with the move from Benfica

But João was captivated by the new direction his football was taking under Simeone, and over the next few weeks he began to settle more.

It quickly became clear to him why Atlético had a reputation as one of the most disciplined sides in Europe.

The whole of today's training session for example had just been spent on defending.

In Simeone's view every player should be able to function as a defender. The position you played on the pitch just defined which areas of the pitch you defended.

João was focusing much more on skills that he'd never really spent enough time on before – such as how to close down the opposition, how to tackle properly, and what his position should be when his team lost the ball.

Then the session turned to another, less well-known (but no less important) aspect of Atlético's game – the dark arts.

This was something that João was still getting his head around.

"Remember, if a guy gets a booking," Simeone explained, "you keep pressing him. You clip his ankles. You tug at his shirt. You shout in his face. You do all you can to wind him up and force him to make a mistake – a mistake that in this case will get him sent off."

João looked around at the other players in the session, still a little shocked that he was hearing this kind of thing being talked about so openly.

"Then, if he touches you, you go down," Simeone continued. "And when you go down, you make sure that the ref sees it – and sees what happened."

João's obvious shock caught the attention of Diego Costa.

"Don't worry yourself, João," the striker growled

reassuringly. "There are rules to the game, and the ref decides if the rules are broken or not. If a guy gets sent off, well, he's broken the rules of the game. That's it – it's that simple."

Diego grinned, then continued. "Every player knows these tricks, and every club wants their players to do these things. The boss here is a just a little more direct in making sure that we're the best at it."

Minutes later, Simeone was setting up a drill for when Atlético went 1-0 up in a game. He was talking Kieran Trippier through how to take a throw-in slowly enough to waste some time, but not so slowly that the ref would actually book him.

João shook his head and marched onto the pitch. *Welcome to top-level football*, he thought.

But if it got results, then that was what mattered.

There was another pressure on João too.

The hype around him had kept on building since he'd joined Atlético. From a player who'd cost nothing and had the safety net of being a home-grown academy talent, he was now the big-money star player who had to deliver.

On top of all that, the manager had also handed João the number 7 shirt – the shirt that had previously been worn by Antoine Griezmann.

These were big shoes to fill – and to cap it all, Simeone had made it clear that Atlético were on a trophy hunt this season.

João would need to deliver on his record-breaking fee.

17
EXHAUSTED

September 2019, Estadio de Anoeta, San Sebastián, Spain
Real Sociedad v Atlético

They were only an hour into the game, but already João was exhausted.

The season had started well for Atlético, with a pre-season destruction of Real Madrid followed by a strong run of wins.

João had settled into the team and was being used mostly as a striker in a rigid 4-4-2, alongside either

Álvaro Morata or Diego Costa. They would occupy the defenders and then João would drop deep, finding the pockets of space he needed to make the most of his pace and his dribbling ability.

It was proving very effective.

"We've found our perfect Griezmann replacement," Saúl joked one day, as they came off the pitch after another win. "Maybe the money they paid for you wasn't a waste after all, João," he joked.

João had been carried through the first few games by the adrenaline of playing in a new team.

There were new faces around him, new tactics and new challenges, and on top of that he'd been buoyed by the energy of the Atlético crowd.

But today, against Real Sociedad, it was all suddenly catching up with him.

Football in the Spanish La Liga was quicker and more physical than in the Primeira Liga, and Atlético were a team that worked hard on the pitch, pressing all the time.

It was all proving to be too much for João and today he was really feeling the effects.

"João!" Costa roared at him. "Keep working! Chase him! Close him down!"

João didn't even have the energy to shout back at Costa. Minutes later he was hauled off, replaced by Ángel Correa.

Simeone didn't say anything as he came off, but João could sense his disappointment.

How could he not be disappointed? They'd paid 126 million for a player who hadn't even lasted an hour on the pitch.

Atlético ended up losing the game 2-0 and João couldn't help but feel that he'd let the team down.

The same thing happened again and again over the following few weeks.

João scored in a win against Mallorca, but in every match he was struggling to last the full 90 minutes, and he was often brought off early.

"What's going on with you, João?" asked Simeone, pulling him aside at the end of one of Atlético's training sessions. "Those first few games you played were vibrant, energetic … You were stunning! I really thought you were going to get 20 goals this season, but you've really slowed down in the last few games."

"I'm just struggling with the pace of it all, boss" João admitted.

He hated to look weak in front of Simeone, but he couldn't keep pretending everything was fine when it plainly wasn't.

"OK, well, we'll get you putting a bit more work in in the gym," Simeone said. "It's always tough adapting to a new league, I know. But look, just so you know – you've got the full support of everyone here at the club. We believe in you, João and we're behind you all the way."

João nodded. At least felt good knowing that the coaching staff still had faith in him.

That night, at he lay in bed, João thought about the conversation he'd had with Simeone.

João wasn't really convinced it was all just a fitness issue.

Deep down, he still had doubts about his abilities. Did he really belong at this level? Was he really worth over 100 million euros?

In his heart, a part of him was thinking that he should have stayed at Benfica.

Everybody was just expecting too much.

18
MORE WOES

November 2019, Nuevo Estadio de Los Cármenes
Granada, Spain, Granada v Atlético

"OK, João. On you go. Let's see how it goes." Simeone looked on as João ran nervously onto the pitch.

They were 75 minutes into the game against Granada, and this was João's first outing in a match, after missing six games with an ankle injury.

Simeone was just giving him a quarter of an hour at the end of the game, to see how things went.

But as soon as he started to play, João could sense that something still wasn't right.

Every movement was painful and slow, and he didn't have the confidence to put his full weight on the ankle.

Worse, he couldn't turn quickly – worrying, because his game often hinged on quickly changing direction.

And he'd lost his touch, and his passing was sloppy.

João was sure that if Simeone had the option, he'd have subbed him straight off again.

João wasn't the only one who was finding things difficult. Atlético continued to struggle, both in La Liga and in the Champions League.

A defeat to Juventus had left them facing a drop down into the Europa League, and they'd also been comfortably beaten by Barcelona, even if the scoreline had only been 1-0.

João knew that he'd often struggled with his confidence in the past, but even so he found it hard not to blame himself for Atlético's woes.

He was their new man, the player that Atlético had

spent a small fortune on, the player that all the fans looked to to lift Atlético to great new heights.

But first it was issues with fitness – or was it more than that? – and now injury.

It seemed as if he was only dragging Atlético down.

19
THE ATLÉTICO WAY

November 2019, Atlético Madrid training ground
Madrid, Spain

João had really struggled to fit in with Atlético's way of playing, but at last he was beginning to think he was getting there.

He always found it toughest in training sessions like today's, when he wasn't simply playing football.

When he was playing football his natural talents could just take over and everything became instinctive.

But, to him, training sessions always seemed to be about drills, tactics, mind games and set-pieces, and this was when he found it hardest to work out what was expected of him.

At Atlético, being very physical – almost aggressive – seemed to be part of their game, but this wasn't João's natural style.

As João went through his drills today, he thought back to the recent Spanish Super Cup game against Barcelona.

Atlético had beaten Barcelona 3-2 in the semi-finals, in a hugely dramatic game. João hadn't scored, but during the game he'd been involved in an angry exchange with several of the Barcelona players.

This was really out of character for him, and he hadn't been particularly proud of the way he'd behaved.

But after the match Simeone had been really ecstatic.

"João, that was brilliant!" he'd said at full time, after Atlético had won the game. "The way you wound them up at half-time! It was great!"

João had laughed along with his boss, but he still wasn't sure if what he'd done had been a good thing.

João wasn't really an aggressive player, but perhaps it was a sign that he was starting to get into the Atlético way of doing things.

Then, off the pitch, João won a major individual award – the Golden Boy Award.

In the past the likes of Messi, Agüero and Mbappé had all collected the trophy. It was a massive vote of confidence for such a younger player.

"Don't let it go to your head," Diego Costa warned him in the training session straight after the award had been announced. "You're not the golden boy here."

Costa was right.

João might be settling more into the Atlético way, but he was still struggling to work out what was expected of him on the pitch.

Simeone never seemed sure how to use him – sometimes as a striker, sometimes a winger.

João always felt he played best up front, alongside another striker, where he had the freedom to drop deep and find the space that allowed him to be so deadly.

But often he seemed to be getting a variety of different and conflicting instructions from the manager.

It was, he thought, partly why he was so mentally and physically exhausted.

20
TURNING POINT

December 2019, Wanda Metropolitano Stadium, Madrid, Spain
Atlético vs Lokomotiv Moscow

As João looked at the team sheet for the game, he was very surprised to see himself down to start.

João had every reason to expect to be on the bench. He'd only recently come back from injury and he still wasn't playing at all well.

He hadn't got any goals – or assists – since October, and he'd never looked like a real threat on the pitch.

But, most important, this wasn't a game that they could afford to lose. In fact they desperately needed a win.

Atlético were playing Lokomotiv Moscow at home in the Champions League. If they won, they'd seal their place in the last 16. But if they lost, and if Bayer Leverkusen got a result, then Atlético would be out.

João knew that normally this would be an easy game, but the way this season had gone so far, he wondered if they could do it.

And he wondered if *he* could do it.

As the Atlético players gathered in the dressing room before the game, Simeone pulled João aside.

"Look João," he said. "I know you've had a tough time of it over the last few weeks. Injury is never easy to get over – it's a mental, as well as a physical thing."

Simeone looked at the young player with that intense gaze of his. "You need to know we're with you on this. All the way. You're going to be back scoring goals in no time."

João found it inspiring to see this normally angry and passionate man being so calm and considerate, especially before a big game like this.

"Thanks, boss," he said. "You know I'll always give it all I've got."

João knew he had to put all his self-doubts behind him.

His team needed him for this game and he needed to do his job, even if he couldn't yet match the fitness of the rest of the team.

João's thoughts were interrupted by shouts of encouragement from the dressing room.

"Come on, lads! We can get this one!" roared Saúl. "The Champions League needs us, and we owe this one to our fans. Let's go and win it!"

Despite the tough times the Atlético players had been through recently, they responded with rousing cheers.

João was playing alongside Álvaro Morata up front and, after only two minutes, with Morata holding onto the ball at the edge of the box, João saw his opportunity.

"Álvaro! In here!" he screamed.

It wasn't a very accurate pass from Morata, and although the ball somehow squirmed into the box, it was a long way from João.

João saw the Lokomotiv keeper going for it, so he quickly sprinted towards the ball – he knew he could get to it before the keeper.

João was right. He got there first and flicked the ball away, but the keeper stuck out a hand, catching João's ankle and bringing him down.

"Penalty!" shouted one of the players behind João.

It was an obvious pen and the ref gave it straight away.

João wanted to take it, but Kieran Trippier was already lining up for it instead.

João watched with the rest of the team as Kieran's weak shot was palmed away by the Lokomotiv keeper.

It was a waste of a great opportunity.

The score was stuck at 0-0.

Play restarted and soon it was clear that João had got his form back. He was at his electric best, turning, spinning, dribbling, passing – and the defenders couldn't touch him.

After 17 minutes Atlético got a second penalty for a handball.

João wasn't going to let this one get away.

"I'm having it. This one's mine," he said confidently.

It was a big moment for Atlético – but it was an even bigger moment for João.

He knew that if he missed this pen, it would be a massive setback in his Atlético career.

Something he might not ever bounce back from.

He breathed out deeply, took a step forward and then hit it low along the ground, to the keeper's right.

The goalkeeper didn't move and the ball whistled past him into the back of the net.

GOAL!

João didn't celebrate wildly. He just pumped his fist and stared up to the sky.

He felt relief as much as anything. The goal was important to Atlético – it may have kept them in the Champions League.

But it was way more important for João. It showed that he still had it.

He could still do this.

João continued his stunning form into the second half.

He didn't score any more goals or get any assists, but he knew he was playing some of his best football ever.

Atlético eventually ran out 2-0 winners, and as João walked off the pitch at the end of the game, he knew it was a significant moment.

It felt like a turning point in his Atlético career.

He was back.

21

DUMPING OUT THE CHAMPIONS

March, 2020, Anfield, Liverpool, England
Champions League Last 16, Liverpool v Atlético

Anfield. Just the name itself was enough to strike fear in the hearts of visiting teams.

Injury had forced João to miss the first leg of this Champions League last 16 game against Liverpool.

Atlético had won it 1-0, but now they were at Anfield for the return leg.

Liverpool had thrashed Barcelona 4-0 here last

season, so the Atlético players knew it was going to be a near impossible task to get through to the next stage, let alone win here.

Simeone performed his usual magic before the game, with a rousing pep talk.

"They've got weaknesses alright, lads, and we've studied them in detail," he said. "So don't forget the game plan – and don't let the crowd get to you. If we ride out the first 30 minutes, we'll be fine."

João started up front alongside Diego Costa.

For João, today wasn't about his attacking ability – it was about how he defended.

That, he knew, was the Atlético way.

He had to hold his shape and prevent Liverpool from starting attacks.

He was going to work harder than ever before, but at the same time he wasn't going to exhaust himself running around chasing the ball.

He was going to conserve his energy for when they did get moments forward.

He had to be ready to play the right pass, take the right shot.

Atlético rode out the first 30 minutes with their 1-0 lead intact, just as Simeone had planned.

But, moments before half-time, disaster struck.

A cross from Alex Oxlade-Chamberlain was met by the head of Gini Wijnaldum.

The ball bounced past Atlético's keeper Oblak and into the net.

It was 1-1, but Atlético were still well in the tie.

The game had already been full of drama, but plenty more was to come.

João saw a shot palmed away, then Atlético had a goal disallowed, and all the while Oblak was masterful, pulling off save after save after save.

But after 90 minutes the score was still 1-0 on the night – 1-1 on aggregate – and the game was going into extra time.

"We're still in this boys, alright?" Simeone roared as the Atlético players gathered together after the 90 minutes.

"We just need one goal – and when we've got that, then they'll need to get two more to win it. So that one goal is all we need."

But then, just three minutes into extra time, it went wrong for Atlético.

Roberto Firmino poked Liverpool into a 2-0 lead.

Moments later, Atlético got their chance.

A poor clearance by Liverpool keeper Adrian fell straight to João's feet. The keeper was off his line, and for a moment João thought about the shot.

But he spotted Marcos Llorente, who'd started a run, so João slipped it into the midfielder, who almost lost it.

For a moment it looked as if the chance was gone. But then Llorente dug the ball out from under his feet and pounced with a low finish into the far corner.

GOAL!

Atlético had their away goal. Now Liverpool needed a third goal to get it back.

"We're back in this, lads," Saúl shouted from midfield. "Dig deep and it's ours!"

João's race was run, though. He was subbed off for Álvaro Morata and he slumped onto the bench, exhausted.

He'd given everything he could – it was up to the others now.

Simeone marched over to him and João thought for a moment that he was going to get a telling off.

"You were brilliant out there, son," Simeone said, sitting himself down next to João. "You were absolutely fantastic, and if you weren't so exhausted, I'd have played you the whole game."

The two Atlético subs turned out to be brilliant. Morata set up Llorente, who made it 2-2, before Morata himself sealed a third.

The game was won!

Atlético had beaten Liverpool 3-2, – 4-2 on aggregate – dumping out the European champions on their own ground.

"You were great today, man," João said, congratulating Oblak on the number of remarkable saves he'd made. "You kept us in this game – we'd have got nowhere without you."

"Thanks. But don't underestimate yourself, João," Oblak replied. "You were amazing out there. You're really starting to find your feet here. I can't wait to see what you do in the rest of this season."

João felt proud. He knew that Oblak was right – he

really was, finally, starting to understand the Atlético spirit and the way they played.

He couldn't wait to continue his development here. He was hungry for the successes that were yet to come.

22
LOCKDOWN

April 2020, João's home, Madrid, Spain

João was glad he'd installed a well-equipped gym in his Madrid home when he'd first moved in.

Now it was really paying off.

Just after Atlético's famous win at Anfield, there had been huge changes in the world of football.

The season had been brought to a sudden halt by COVID-19 and all La Liga games had been cancelled.

João had joined footballers around the world in self-isolating at home, unable to play the sport that he loved.

Simeone wasn't at all put off by the fact that his players were now stuck inside.

He saw COVID as an opportunity, and had them all on a strict training schedule, keen to ensure that when they returned they were ready to hit the ground running.

It wasn't ideal for João, who'd only just started to bond with his new teammates and now suddenly found himself unable to see them on a daily basis.

But he was able to turn the lockdown to his advantage as well.

It was a chance to rest physically and to recover his mental strength and enthusiasm for the game.

When matches resumed again in June, João knew he was ready.

It was good to see the Atlético boys again, and his enthusiasm to get back to playing games was matched by the rest of the squad.

For the first time in a while, the Atlético players felt they had the right balance between young, attacking talents and the experienced old heads.

They were ready to win.

23

NEVER AGAIN

August 2020, Estádio José Alvalade, Lisbon, Portugal
RB Leipzig vs Atlético, Champions League quarter-final

João couldn't wait to get going. Because of COVID, the Champions League was a mini-tournament this year, beginning in August, after the league season had finished.

Atlético's first match was their quarter-final against RB Leipzig.

João had picked up an ankle injury in the closing weeks of the season, but now he was fit and raring to go.

He knew the eyes of the world were on this tournament and he was desperate to impress.

"I'm sorry, João, but you're on the bench for this one," Simeone told him the night before the match. "Marcos Llorente has been in great form as a striker and we're going to need his defensive stability in midfield."

Shocked, João didn't say anything.

He knew better than to question Simeone, but he couldn't hide the disappointment that was written all over his face.

"I promise you, I'll get you on," Simeone said, putting an arm around João's shoulder. "You won't spend the whole game on the sidelines."

The first twenty minutes were quiet and João found himself constantly glancing over to Simeone. He was itching to play.

After a dull first half, João waited patiently in the dressing room for Simeone to get him on. Surely he couldn't leave him on the bench, the way Atlético were playing.

But the call never came.

Five minutes into the second half, Leipzig took the lead.

Ten minutes after that, Simeone finally relented and João found himself stepping out onto the pitch, taking the place of Héctor Herrera.

João was determined to prove himself, to prove to Simeone that he should have brought him on sooner.

He was constantly running at defenders, causing chaos in the Leipzig team. They were terrified of him and always backed off.

Each time it happened, João's confidence grew.

Twenty minutes into the second half, João played a sharp one-two with Diego Costa and burst into the box. He saw the goal opening up and pulled his foot back. But as he did, João felt his legs swept from under him.

"Ref!" he yelled, as he fell forward onto the floor.

It was a simple decision for the referee and he pointed straight to the penalty spot.

João was not going to let anyone else take this. He stood next to the ball with a determined look in his eye, ready to take on any Atlético players who might try and take this penalty off him.

But it seemed that everyone could sense his attitude. Nobody tried to stop him. This was his.

João took two steps and blasted it to the keeper's right. The keeper went the right way, but he was too slow. The ball nestled in the back of the net.

GOAL!

João raced after it and grabbed it, sprinting back to the half-way line.

There was no time for celebrations. There were twenty minutes left in the game for Atlético to try and grab a winner.

João tried his best, working desperately to get the goal they needed, but it was no use. Leipzig were the better team and they had the better chances. It took a long time, but Leipzig finally got their winner in the 88th minute.

Atlético were out of the Champions League.

After twelve long months, the season was finally over. Atlético – and João – had finished it trophyless.

At full time, Simeone was seething. "Don't forget what happened here, boys," he roared. "Next year we're going for the title – and we won't have anything like this happen again."

24
BACK IN STYLE

December, 2020, Wanda Metropolitano Stadium
Madrid, Spain, Atlético v Bayern Munich

As João sat in the dressing room and tried to get used to the unusual quiet – matches were still being played to empty stadiums – he smiled as he thought about his first meeting with Atlético's new striker.

Luis Suárez had joined Atlético over the summer from Barcelona, in what had been a huge move.

João had met a number of top players in his short

career so far, but he'd felt as nervous about talking to Suárez as he'd felt when he'd first met Ronaldo in his early days in the Portugal squad.

As it turned out, Suárez had wasted no time in meeting his fellow striker.

"You're João, right?" he'd said, a wide smile on his face. "I think we're playing up front together this year."

João had nodded.

"I've seen a bit of you," Luis had continued. "You remind me a lot of Leo."

"Leo Messi?" João had asked, not quite believing that he was being compared to one of the best players of all time.

"Yeah. The way you run with the ball, it's a bit like him."

"Thank you," was all João had said.

"We're going to score goals together this year, João. The defenders are going to come for me, and you're going to have so much space … You'll just need to make the most of it."

So far Suárez had been proved right.

João had scored five times in Atlético's opening nine

games of the season, with the club making an unbeaten start to the season and racing to the top of the league. They were now well in the title race and still undefeated in the league.

But today's game was in the Champions League, against the current European champions Bayern Munich.

Atlético hadn't seen the same success in Europe, and they needed to win this game to be sure of staying in the competition.

"This is it, lads," Simeone said, standing tall in the dressing room and instantly grabbing the player's attention. "We lose this and we might be out of the Champions League – again! So you know what you have to do."

"We've proved ourselves in the league, boys," captain Koke added. "Now it's time to send a message to the rest of Europe that we mean business."

There was always pressure before a big match, especially a Champions League game against a team like Bayern, but today there was a huge extra pressure on João.

Suárez was out, injured, so Atlético were looking to João to dominate up front and get their goals.

Atlético started strongly, with João at the very centre of things. It was his slipped pass that found the feet of Ángel Correa, but the striker scuffed his shot and it found the keeper.

"You're quicker than the defenders, João!" Kieran Trippier shouted to him. "If you get in front of them, they'll have to foul you – they won't get back round."

Moments later, Marcos Llorente burst down the right-hand side. João was the first to react, sprinting past the motionless Bayern defenders.

By the time they realised what was happening, it was too late.

Llorente's cross was inch-perfect and João was there to smash the ball past the helpless Alexander Nübel in goal.

GOAL!

"When we've got João we don't even need Suárez!" Llorente shouted, as the players celebrated in front of the empty stadium.

For the next hour, Atlético held on to their 1-0 lead.

João almost doubled their lead with a brilliant chance, but he smashed the ball against the crossbar and the rebound didn't quite fall for him.

But then, just four minutes from time, a clumsy foul at the other end gave Thomas Müller an opportunity to equalise from the penalty spot.

The German duly converted it and Bayern were able to hold on for a point in a 1-1 draw.

It wasn't the result that Atlético had wanted, but it did keep them in the competition.

But for João it was much more than that.

On the biggest stage, and against the best team in Europe, he had quite simply been the star of the show, running the game from start to finish.

After a quiet first year, João had signalled his return to the very top.

25

CHAMPIONS OF SPAIN

May 2021, José Zorrilla Stadium, Valladolid, Spain
Valladolid v Atlético

As the full-time whistle blew, the Atlético players raised their arms in victory, huge smiles on all their faces.

João looked up at the huge contingent of Atlético fans that had made the trip to Valladolid for this massive game today.

The final score was 2-1 to Atlético, and with that result they had just clinched the Spanish league title, finishing two points ahead of defending champions Real Madrid.

"I told you João, remember?"

João turned to see Luis Suárez beaming at him. "I said we were going to score a lot of goals together this year. And just look what we've done! La Liga is ours!"

It was Atlético's first title win in seven years, beating both Real Madrid and Barcelona – a massive achievement given that the league was dominated year after year by these two wealthy clubs.

Simeone was already on the pitch too, running from one Atlético player to the next, hugging them, congratulating them, celebrating the title win.

"I said we'd do it!" he shouted to his players. "I told you, this year we'd get the title. And you've not let me down."

João sank to his knees, not sure how to celebrate. It was his first Spanish title, but for him it was so much more than that.

He thought back to the day when he'd decided to leave Benfica to move to Atlético. It had been a tough decision, but he remembered thinking on that day about

Ronaldo, and how he'd won the league in three different countries in Europe.

That was when João had made that same achievement his dream too, and he'd joined Atlético to help make the dream become a reality.

And now he was here, the winner of league titles in Portugal, with Benfica, and in Spain, with Atlético.

Now he felt sure he could do the same anywhere he played football, whether he was playing for club or for country.

The future was his for the making – he simply felt unstoppable.

And he'd only just turned 21.

HOW MANY
HAVE YOU READ?

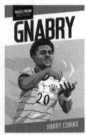

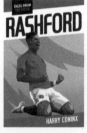